healing. growth. self-discovery.

*To my inner child,
you are so loved.*

TABLE OF

CONTENTS

1000 journal prompts.

healing. growth. self-discovery.

- prithvi madhukar -

NOTE TO THE JOURNALER

Hi there, I'm Prithvi! I'm so happy you've picked my journal prompts book to help you with your self-love journey.

I thought I'd give you a small insight into the inspiration behind this book. The story is pretty interesting!

I completed my engineering degree only to realize my passion for marketing. After choosing to follow my passion and completing an MBA with a concentration in Marketing in New York, I worked at a top solar firm in the state for a year.

Here's a plot twist: My H-1B work visa did not process, and I was forced to leave the US. This meant I had to leave my fantastic full-time job, amazing colleagues, best friends, and a place I had called home for three years.

I was devastated and desperate to find hope in life again. In 2019, I decided to risk my entire savings and invest in my dream of becoming a digital entrepreneur. The decision came from extreme anger, anguish, and pain. At this point in my life, I had been through a decade of constant hits from life, and frankly, this was my last straw. I couldn't understand why life was so hard on me, and if this was all that life was about, then I didn't see the point of living it.

My mental and emotional health had deteriorated significantly by this point, and as more time passed, I could see that it was also affecting my business. I decided to invest time and determine why my life had spun out of control. I also wanted to know how to bring my life back to where I could manage it.

The more I looked back at the decade of hits that life had given me, the more I started to understand that it stemmed from decisions that came from a place of pain and unhealed wounds. The problems seemed so complex and out of my control at first glance, but the more I dug into them, the more I realized that it came down to one simple thing: *I did not know how to love myself.*

And thus, I began my self-love and healing journey. I do not know how I had such faith that this was the only way to turn my life around, but I'm so glad I took on the responsibility of learning to love myself.[1]

As part of my journey, I started journaling. At first, my entries were just random thoughts running in my head that needed an outlet. Over time and consistent journaling, my journal entries became much more

---

[1] If you want the full story, along with 60 stories and lessons about my entrepreneurial journey then, check out my debut book: Zero to Four Figures: Lessons Learned by a Broke CEO https://www.themarketingnomad.co/books/zerotofourfigures

structured. They focused on a particular topic, and I would take the time to analyze, dissect, and revise my thought process based on where I was at that point in my life. It's been a few years since I began my self-love and healing journey, and I am amazed that I could turn my life around, simply by looking inward.

In November 2022, a tweet of mine when viral. I wrote, "Everyone talks about trauma healing, but no one ever talks about the guilt we feel when we wish to bring someone into a life we have spent healing from."

I was amazed at how many people it resonated with. The more I researched, the more I realized that there are so many little repercussions of trauma that we don't recognize and don't think too much of, even though the impact of it on our lives is huge.

I looked at how I captured these little behaviors of mine and realized it all came from years of journaling. I wanted to help more people feel seen, but I didn't know how. I wasn't comfortable sharing my experiences given its sensitivity and my need for privacy, but at the same time, I wanted to help people with their self-love journey in the best way I could.

In February 2023, the inspiration hit—Journal Prompts!

I was SO excited about the idea, and I immediately got to work. I combed through all my journal entries since 2019 and categorized them. I reverse-engineered my journal entries to create a series of prompts from them. Additionally, I tapped into my empathy to incorporate prompts inspired by the life lessons I had gathered from my surroundings over the years. It took me a few months as I had other verticals of my Marketing Consultancy business to run. I ended up with 1000 journal prompts, and trust me, there is NO ONE more surprised than me, haha!

It is my absolute privilege and honor to share those 1000 journal prompts with you. I hope it shows you, just as it continues to show me, that self-love is the MOST powerful thing in the world, and it is what will bring you the life you wish for.

Now, I have a few other things for you to keep in mind as you are working through the journal prompts:

No Particular Order

You can choose whichever topic you'd like to write. You don't have to go in the order that I've placed the topics or even the individual journal prompts.

No Need to Send the Letters

Some journal prompts are about writing letters to specific people in your life. You don't have to send or show those letters to the person if you don't want to. The prompts are to help you put your thoughts, feelings, and emotions onto paper.

Relationships

Unless specifically mentioned, the term 'relationships' defines any relationship like platonic, familial, work, romantic, etc. You can choose to interpret the prompt in any or all ways.

Not a Substitute for Professional Help

I wrote this book to share what has helped me on my journey of self-love and healing. I hope you can use it as a starting point for yours. However, it is important to understand that I'm neither a licensed therapist nor a trained psychologist. Each person's journey is unique, so please don't use this book as a substitute for professional help. If you find yourself in need of help, I strongly encourage you to seek it.

Additionally, I want to highlight that you can use these questions and prompts as a foundation for discussions with a professional. If you're working with a licensed therapist or other qualified mental health experts, these questions/prompts could complement your conversations and aid your healing and self-love process.

No Right or Wrong Answers

The prompts are for you to view your genuine thoughts and feelings. Sometimes, they may not be what you hope to think and feel. That's completely okay. Part of the self-love process is to embrace ALL of you, *the true you.* There are no right or wrong answers with self-reflection.

Be Authentic

The goal is to heal, grow and discover yourself. The people around you may have their own opinions, and sometimes, you may feel pressured to follow their thoughts/feelings. Do your best to resist the urge and stay true to yourself–What do YOU think? What do YOU feel? What do YOU want?

Safe Space

I cannot stress this enough–The first thing you must do is create a safe space for yourself. I like to call it the "No Judgement Zone." As you work through your thoughts, feelings, emotions, and past experiences, a lot of new realizations will come to the surface. Don't judge yourself, don't focus on the perceived shortcomings, don't criticize yourself, and don't form a negative opinion of yourself. You must also be incredibly kind towards yourself and recognize that this is natural part of the human experience.

Take Your Time / Trigger Warning

There is no deadline to finish the journal prompts in this book. I know it may feel silly for me to bring it up, but in our hurry to heal, we may sometimes feel the urge to finish all the prompts. The truth is that sometimes, the prompt may trigger you in a healthy way, and you may need some time to cool off, collect your thoughts and regulate your emotions. It's absolutely okay. Take your time with the prompts. You don't have to finish writing your answer within a set time. *Ironically, hurrying slows the healing process.* So, take a deep breath, and work through the prompts at your own pace.

Keep Connecting
These prompts are just a starting point for you. If it kickstarts other thoughts, keep connecting them. Don't be afraid to keep adding tangents. Keep going where your thoughts take you!

Revisit & Review
I know it can be a little hard to review older journal entries because of the feelings/emotions they can bring up, but if you feel up to it, take the time to review. Take a look at your older journal entries with the knowledge you have gained in the time that has passed. If new feelings/emotions come up, take the time to write and reflect on those as well. Remember, healing is before, after, and everything in between. It is fluid, meaning it has no start or end point. In my opinion, the best way to approach healing is to flow with it; with no beginning or end, but just going where it takes you.

Find Comfort in the Process
I agree that some of the prompts in this book are deeper and require you to reach within the depths of your journey thus far, but that does not mean you shouldn't find comfort in the process.

You are a beautiful and unique human. You are a gift, yes you, exactly as you are. I hope you recognize that getting to know YOU is a privilege, and every moment of it must be cherished.

Take care and all the very best!

Lots of love,

Prithvi Madhukar, aka The Marketing Nomad

DAILY
GRATITUDE

Importance:

When I started journaling, I was deep in my victim mindset and struggled to find hope for a better tomorrow. I felt that life was constantly out to get me, and I kept worrying about how much worse my life could get.

Based on the many recommendations I saw online, I decided to practice daily gratitude. Each day, I would find one thing that I was grateful for. I will admit it was hard at first. I was so resentful that appreciating what I had was the furthest from my mind. But I persisted.

I started with small things. Grateful for my post-it notes, grateful for my phone, grateful for my water bottle. Over time, I moved on to bigger things. Grateful for something that made me laugh, grateful for my life experiences, grateful for the people in my life.

I have to say this practice completely transformed my outlook on life over time. It forced me to focus on what I did have instead of what I didn't. The happier I felt when I recognized something that I did have, the more enthusiastic I was to find more. Without me realizing it, this practice put me in an abundance mindset and made me more conscious of everything I was blessed with. Soon, I became content with what I had and believed that all I had was enough to transform my life.

And what do ya know, it did. :)

Journal Structure:

Here are some additional questions to help you structure each journal entry after you've picked a prompt to work on:

- Why are you grateful for it?
- What difference has it made to your life?
- How different would your life be without it?
- How is your life better off with it?
- Do you have any other memories associated with it?
- How can you continue to be grateful for it?
- What intentional actions can you take to express your gratitude or to remind yourself to be grateful for it?
- How can you use what you are grateful for to make your life better?

Focus on what you do have,

and you'll realize

it is plenty to begin with.

Write about the time you laughed till you cried.	What made you chuckle today?	What is an item you use everyday that seems insignificant but you would not be able to function without it?
Who was there for you when you needed a shoulder to cry on?	What do you have today that you once prayed for?	What is the most thoughtful gift you have ever received?

DAILY GRATITUDE

How do your loved ones show they care about you?	What is the kindest thing a stranger has done for you?	Name the people in your life who you are grateful for and write why.
What made you smile today?	Write about the best meal you have ever had in your life.	What did you have as a child that you are grateful for today?

What is the most selfless thing someone has done for you?	Write about a time when a family member helped you through a difficult situation.	Write about a time when your family / family member encouraged you.
Which family tradition(s) are you grateful for?	Write about the best memory you have with your family / family member(s).	Write about the time a family member gave you guidance.

DAILY GRATITUDE

Write about an inside joke in your family that always cracks you up.	Write about a family member who always has your back.	Write about a time your family / family member supported you in your life decisions / choices.
Write about a time your family / family member cared about your needs.	Write about a time your family / family member went out of their way to let you know they love you.	Write about a time your family / family member appreciated you.

What is one good quality of yours that you attribute to your upbringing?	What is the best thing about your family?	Write about a time your pet made you laugh.
Write about a time your pet showed you unconditional love.	What is the best thing about your pet?	What has your pet taught you?

DAILY GRATITUDE

Write about a time your pet comforted you.	Write about a time your pet helped you through a rough time.	Write about a friend who has always been there for you.
Write about a friend who has always supported you.	Write about a time when a friend encouraged you.	Write about a time when a friend showed they cared about you.

What difference has good health brought to your life?	Write about how your body, mind, soul have contributed to the life you live today.	What freedom has your good health given you?
Write about all the daily functions your body allows you to do.	Write all the positive things about your body. *(Take the time to observe yourself in the mirror with kindness, compassion and most importantly, with no judgement.)*	What has good health allowed you to experience?

DAILY GRATITUDE

What has good health allowed you to practice?	What has good health allowed you to create?	Write about why you love your home.
What has your home provided you with?	Write about the best memories you have had in your home.	Write about an item / room / space in your home that brings the fondest memories for you.

Write about a time your education helped you out of a sticky situation.

What important life lessons has your education taught you?

What important life skills has your education taught you?

What opportunities has your education unlocked for you?

What new experiences has your education given you?

How has your education helped you in your career?

DAILY GRATITUDE

Write about the time you had a good night's sleep.

Write about the difference you feel when you get a good night's sleep.

Which is your favorite season and why are you grateful for it?

Write a few good things about your financial situation that you are grateful for.

What life lessons has your financial situation taught you?

What can you afford today, that you couldn't before?

Write about one thing you have right now that money cannot buy.	Describe the freedom your financial situation has given you.	Write about someone who taught you a very important life lesson.
Write about a teacher who had a positive and big impact on your life.	Write about a teacher who inspired you to unlock your potential.	Write about a book that changed your life.

DAILY GRATITUDE

Write about a book that you immensely enjoyed.	Write about a good hair day.	What do you like about your hair? What makes your hair unique?
What is your favorite feature about yourself?	Write about a solo road trip that changed your life and why you are grateful for it.	Write about the best road trip you have ever been on and why you are grateful for it.

What has Time taught you and why are you grateful for it?	What has Time allowed you to do and why are you grateful for it?	Write about how grateful you are when someone set aside time just for you.
What is the best gift that Time has given you and why are you grateful for it?	Which is your favorite footwear and why are you grateful for it?	Write about a time you received a heartfelt apology and why you are grateful for it.

DAILY GRATITUDE

Write about a time you had a good, long, late night conversation and why you are grateful for it.	Write about a time when you changed your perspective on something and why you are grateful for it.	Write about a time you felt a sense of accomplishment when you checked off everything on your to-do list.
Write about a time when a choice you made resulted in something positive.	What has diversity taught you and why are you grateful for it?	Write about a place you visited and how it changed you.

Write about a time when your hard work paid off.	What has Pain taught you and how can you exercise healthy gratitude towards it?	What are the current challenges in your life teaching you and how can you exercise healthy gratitude towards it?

DAILY GRATITUDE

Write about a time you were forgiven by someone and why you are grateful for it.	What is your favorite food / cuisine and why are you grateful for it?	Which is your favorite outfit and why are you grateful for it?

SELF-DISCOVERY

Importance:

My self-discovery journey started in 2019, and I've realized this is a lifelong process. Not that I'm complaining, of course. I find it beautiful that there will always be something about myself that is yet to be discovered.

The more I dived into my self-discovery journey, the more I learned the depths of who I was, what I wanted, my beliefs, values, thought processes, perceived flaws, and imperfections. As I continued to discover myself, it gave me the courage to take the steps that resonated with my innermost desires. Over time, those steps, big and small, slowly started to align me with a life that brought me peace.

I'm not saying there aren't conflicts or chaos in my life today; of course, there are! But the more I get to know myself, the more I learn to manage myself. This helps me become more confident in navigating uncomfortable situations.

I know some may be afraid of what they'll find when they keep digging into their imperfections, and frankly, I was too. But when I got to understand parts of myself, yes, even the parts that I perceived were flawed, something amazing happened—I started finding beauty in being exactly the way I was, perceived flaws, imperfections, and all.

The more beauty I recognized in myself, the more beauty I recognized in the people around me. It made me kinder to other people who were doing their best navigating through life, just as I was. It helped me accept people for who they were instead of trying to mold them to fit my perception. It transformed how I showed up in my relationships, and as a result of giving people space to be themselves, my relationship with them became so much more enriching. I credit that to my self-discovery journey, and I hope you too, can experience the same for yourself.

Journal Structure:

Here are some additional questions to help you structure each journal entry after you've picked a prompt to work on:

- Where does that part of you stem from?
- Are there any instances you are reminded of or that showcase that trait of yours?
- How does that trait add value to your life?
- How can you be more accepting of a particular trait / belief / thought process?
- How can you hold onto that part of you? How can you honor what makes you, you?

The most loving thing you can do

for yourself is to answer,

who are you?

Which is your favorite movie and why?

Which is your favorite color and why? What does the color represent to you?

Which is your favorite non-fiction book and why?

Which is your favorite fiction book and why?

Which is your favorite genre and why?

(music / movie / books)

Which is your favorite animal and why?

SELF-DISCOVERY

Which is your favorite country and why?

Do you prefer the beach or the mountains? Why? How does the place make you feel?

Which is your favorite meal time and why?

What kind of food do you prefer having for each meal time and why?

What kind of music do you listen to when you are happy and why?

What kind of music do you listen to when you are sad and why?

Write ten words that best describe you and explain how you embody each word.	How do you perceive accountability? What makes a person accountable?	How do you define ambition? What does ambition mean to you? What is your ambition?
How adaptable are you? Mention instances that support your viewpoint. Is it something you would like to work on?	What do you define as success?	What do you define as a work-life balance?

SELF-DISCOVERY

How important is it to you to be liked by people? List instances that has worked for you, and against you.	How important is it for you to be the best in the room? Write the pros and cons. Is there something you would like to improve / change?	Would you call yourself a caring person? How do you feel about it?
Are you a cautious person? How do you feel about it? Is there something you would like to improve / change?	On a scale of 1-10, how is your clarity of thought? Does it vary in different situations? Why or why not?	What do you define as a commitment from yourself? What do you define as a commitment from someone else?

How do you show up when you have made a commitment? Is there something you would like to change / improve?	On a scale of 1-10, how much do you expect from the people around you and why? Is it healthy?	What do you define as compassion? On a scale of 1-10, how compassionate are you? Is it something you would like to improve / change?
On a scale of 1-10, how competitive are you? Why do you think that is? Is it healthy?	What do you define as healthy competition? How can you foster more of that environment?	How do you resolve conflict? Is it healthy? What can you do differently? How can you improve on your conflict resolution skills?

SELF-DISCOVERY

What are you passionate about? What do you find yourself doing that makes you unimaginably happy?	On a scale of 1-10, how harsh is your inner critic? What can you do to tame your inner critic?	On a scale of 1-10, how self-compassionate are you? What can you do to be more self-compassionate?
What do you define as self-confidence? What are the signs that you exhibit to show you have it?	On a scale of 1-10, how self-confident are you? What can you do to raise your self-confidence?	What do you define as self-discovery? Which parts of yourself would you like to get to know better?

How do you perceive your accomplishments? *(accept them / dismiss them / self-conscious about them, etc)* Why do you think that is?	How do you feel when someone praises you? How do you usually react? Is it healthy? Is there something you would like to change / improve?	Describe Life in 10 separate words. How many are positive and how many negative? How can you have a more healthy perspective about Life?
Do you remember your dreams? Do you believe dreams have meaning? Why or why not?	What do you define as a strength? What are your strengths? List as many as you can.	What do you define as a weakness? What are your weaknesses?

SELF-DISCOVERY

What can you do to overcome your perceived weaknesses?	If you can't overcome your weaknesses *(and that's okay sometimes)*, what can you do to work around them?	On a scale of 1-10, how hard is it to see yourself as beautiful? What mindset shifts can you make so that it becomes easier?
What do you define as a goal? How do you identify a goal for your life? What is your thought process leading up to it? What inspires you to define a goal?	How do you define a short-term goal? What time period equates to a short-term goal for you? What are your short-term goals?	How do you define a long-term goal? What time period equates to a long-term goal for you? What are your long-term goals?

If you had to pick 5 non-materialistic things that matter the most to you, what would they be and why?	If you had to pick 5 materialistic things that matter the most to you, what would they be and why?	What are 5 qualities in a friend that are most important to you and why?
What are 5 qualities in a partner that are most important to you and why?	What are 5 qualities in your child / children that you hope they will have and why?	What are 5 qualities in you that you wish to have for the rest of your life and why?

SELF-DISCOVERY

Which activities are fun for you? What do you enjoy about them?	Which activities are relaxing for you? What do you enjoy about them?	Which activities are stressful for you? Why do you find them stressful?
What do you define as financial stability? How financially stable do you perceive yourself to be? Is it a healthy perception?	What do you define as a family? What do you define as a home?	On a scale of 1-10, how much do you care about the environment? Why or why not?

On a scale of 1-10,
how aware are you
of the happenings
in the world?
Why or why not?

What do you define
as friendship?
Who would you
consider as a friend?

On a scale of 1-10,
how well do you know
about your health?
*(Emotional, physical,
mental, spiritual)*
What steps can
you take to get
to know it better?

What do you define
as independence?
How do you perceive
your independence?

What do you define
as financial
independence?
How do you perceive
your financial
independence?

What kind of
independence
do you wish for?

SELF-DISCOVERY

What do you define
as freedom?
How do you perceive
your freedom?

What do you define
as financial freedom?
How do you perceive
your financial freedom?

What kind of freedom
do you wish for?

What do you define
as forgiveness?

How forgiving are you?
What do you think
is the reason for it?

Can you forgive people
without an apology?
Why or why not?

How important is it for you to be forgiven by someone you love?

How important is it for you to be forgiven by a friend? What do you think is the reason for it?

On a scale of 1-10, how difficult is it for you to recognize that you are in the wrong? What do you think is the reason for it?

On a scale of 1-10, how difficult is it for you to apologize when you are in the wrong? What do you think is the reason for it?

What do you perceive is a good apology?

How do you apologize when you are in the wrong?

SELF-DISCOVERY

How do you feel when you are in the wrong? What are the thoughts in your mind when you are wrong?

How do you feel when you are right? How do you usually react? Is it healthy?

On a scale of 1-10, how often do you follow through on your words? How do you feel about that?

How do you feel when someone tells you that you are wrong? How do you react? Is it healthy?

How do you perceive failure? How do you perceive your failure? How do you perceive someone else's failure?

What are your thoughts when you perceive you have failed? Are they healthy? If not, what can you do to make them healthy?

How do you react when you perceive you have failed? What actions do you take? Are they healthy? If not, what can you do to make them healthy?

How do you feel when someone talks about your past mistakes? How do you react?

How do you feel when someone shames you? How do you react?

SELF-DISCOVERY

How do you feel when someone criticizes you? What is your thought process like?

How do you feel when someone does not acknowledge the work you have done? How do you react?

How do you feel when someone doesn't acknowledge your care, concern and / or love for them? How do you react?

REFLECTIONS

Importance:

I've always liked reflecting on my life. Taking the time to think about what has passed, my thoughts on it, or even thinking about where I am right now and the future I see for myself. Here are a few ways that reflections have helped me:

When I look back at past mistakes, it is not to berate myself but to see how I can use the lessons learned to empower myself for the future.

When I take the time to analyze my current decisions in my life, I'm giving myself a chance to objectively see whether I may have missed something or if there's another, more straightforward way to approach something. Or sometimes, reflecting on my current decisions reinforces that it was the right decision, which gives me the confidence to continue.

When I choose to reflect on the person I am today, it gives me an insight into how my future will be impacted by it. If I find that the future I envision doesn't align with what I desire, I still have the opportunity to make adjustments.

From what I've come to understand, the opportunity to course correct so that you can build a life that aligns with who you are, doesn't materialize on its own. The opportunity needs to be created by us through our reflections and subsequent intentional choices. This is why taking time out of one's life to reflect is important.

As you work through prompts in this chapter, you may find new aspects of your life to reflect on. I would say, go where your thoughts take you. The more tangents you can reflect on, the more information you have on your hand to empower your decision-making process for your life.

Journal Structure:

Here are some additional questions to help you structure each journal entry after you've picked a prompt to work on:

- What thoughts of yours on the prompt are unique?
- What thoughts of yours on the prompt are similar to other people? (This will help you empathize with people and the experiences that they are going through)
- How can you use the thoughts laid out from the prompt to make intentional choices / decisions for your life?

Look back

to empower yourself

as you move forward.

Write about a time you reacted negatively to someone. What should you have done differently?

Write about a time you reacted positively to someone. How can you keep aligning with that?

Write about a time you were surprised by your own behavior. Why did you behave that way? How do you feel about it today?

Write about what you did differently today / this week / this month / this year.

How do you respond to bad news? What can you do differently to receive it in a healthy way?

How do you respond to someone criticizing you? How can you set boundaries and receive it in a healthy way?

REFLECTIONS

How do you respond to someone else's good news?

How do you respond when someone says hurtful things to you? How do you respond when you hear someone has said hurtful things about you to someone else?

How do you behave when you feel stuck? What are the thoughts / actions / feelings you have when you feel stuck?

How do you respond when you are hurt by someone's actions? Is it a healthy response? How would you like to respond?

How do you behave when you are stressed? Is it a healthy response? How would you like to respond?

How do you react when you face a disappointment?

How do you treat
your loved ones?
How can you
treat them better?

Make a list of
your positive
behavioral traits
that you admire
about yourself.

How do you respond
when someone is angry
with you?

If you could
go back in time
to change the way
you behaved
in a particular situation,
what would you
do differently?

What are you
most proud of?

How do you respond
when someone
showers you with
love and affection?

REFLECTIONS

How do you
perceive love?
What do you
define as love?

How do you
show love to yourself?

Objectively view
yourself and describe
who you are.

How do you speak
to yourself?
Is it filled with love?
How would you
like to speak
to yourself?

How can you evolve
the way you speak
to yourself
so that you are more
loving and kind?

How do you feel
about the life you have
lived so far?

How do you feel about the life yet to unfold?	How do you feel about your loved ones? How do you feel about their presence in your life?	How do you feel about your current situation? *(Financial, health, career, personal life, etc)*
What are the recurring thoughts in your mind? Are they healthy? How do you feel about them?	How do you feel about the range of emotions you feel? How do you feel about your emotional intelligence?	What are you thinking about right now?

REFLECTIONS

Notice your actions and feelings right now. Describe them in detail.	Think about any significant life event / incident. What are your thoughts about it? What did you feel about it back then? How do you feel about it now?	Make a list of all the healthy perceptions you have. *(On life, career, finance, love, etc)*
Which attitude is holding you back from achieving success? How would you like to change it?	Which attitude is holding you back from a fulfilling love life? How would you like to change it?	Which attitude is holding you back from achieving financial stability? How would you like to change it?

Which attitude is holding you back from appreciating life? How would you like to change it?

Which attitude is holding you back from trying new things? How would you like to change it?

Which attitude is holding you back from experiencing new friendships? How would you like to change it?

Which attitude is holding you back from accepting your current situation? How would you like to change it?

Which attitude is holding you back from healing your trauma? How would you like to change it?

Which attitude is holding you back from healing your childhood trauma? How would you like to change it?

REFLECTIONS

Which attitude is holding you back from feeling safe and secure in your life? How would you like to change it?

Which attitude is holding you back from being loved by the people around you? How would you like to change it?

Which attitude is holding you back from following your dreams? How would you like to change it?

Which attitude is holding you back from tapping into your potential? How would you like to change it?

Which attitude is holding you back from processing your pain? How would you like to change it?

Which attitude is holding you back from identifying and overcoming your limiting beliefs? How would you like to change it?

Which attitude is holding you back from appreciating the simple pleasures in life?
How would you like to change it?

Which attitude is holding you back from living in the present moment?
How would you like to change it?

Which attitude is holding you back from loving yourself unconditionally?
How would you like to change it?

What are you hopeful for in your career?

What are you hopeful for in your personal life?

What are you hopeful for in your love life?

REFLECTIONS

What are you hopeful for in your current financial situation?

What inspires you to get out of bed?

What are you passionate about and why?

What inspires you to work?

What inspires you to pursue your dreams?

What inspires you to be a better person every day?

What inspires you to be physically fit?	What inspires you to be mentally and emotionally fit?	What inspires you to heal?
What inspires you to show up authentically?	What inspires you to love unconditionally?	What motivates you during tough times?

REFLECTIONS

What motivates you throughout the day?	What inspires you to honor your commitments?	What inspires you to challenge yourself?
What are you seeking from your career?	What are you seeking from life?	What are you seeking from your love life?

What are you seeking from your loved ones?	What are you seeking from your finances?	What do you desire for your loved ones?
What do you desire for yourself?	What do you desire from yourself?	What do you desire from your career?

REFLECTIONS

What do you desire from your peers / colleagues?	What do you desire from life?	What do you desire from your loved ones?
What do you desire from your health?	How can you achieve your desires in each area of your life? What steps can you take?	What will make you feel fulfilled?

What triggers you to have negative thoughts? How can you realign your thoughts to positive ones?

Write about a time you felt a negative emotion. How did you handle it? How could you have handled it better?

According to you, what is the meaning of Life?

REFLECTIONS

How long are you willing to pursue your dreams / desires?

Describe what your dream future looks like.

(in detail)

Why do you desire the things you desire? Where does it stem from? What is the reasoning behind it?

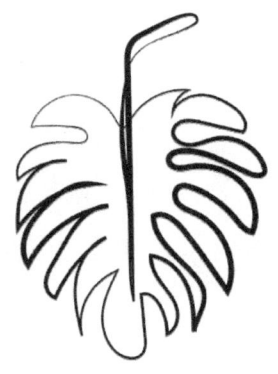

MANIFESTATION

Importance:

I'd like to share my perception of manifestation. Of course, you are free to create your understanding of it too!

For me, I believe in energy. I believe that we attract things of the same frequency as ours. By that, we attract our manifestation only when we are in the same frequency. The longer we stay in that frequency, the closer our manifestation comes to us. The more we are off the frequency, the more delayed our manifestation gets. Following this theory, I believe that if I do my best to embody that frequency and, more importantly, maintain it, the energy I'm in slowly starts aligning me with my manifestation. In other words, I increase the probability of attracting my manifestation and reducing the delay.

So, to me, manifestation is more about my ability to stay in the frequency of what I wish to manifest, which is reflected in my journal entries about manifestation. My journal entries help me maintain that frequency. It enables me to recognize when I'm off, thus allowing me to realign to the frequency of my manifestation.

Now, the frequency of our manifestation can be achieved by gaining clarity on the manifestation, our actions, thoughts, beliefs, and emotions. And sometimes–this may sound wild–it could even be achieved with our inaction, taking a step back, or letting go.

Identifying *how* to embody that frequency is a big part of my journaling process, and now, you can use this technique too!

Journal Structure:

Here are some additional questions to help you structure each journal entry after you've picked a prompt to work on:

- What would you see, think, feel, and smell if you were living your manifestation right now?
- What else surrounds your manifestation? (Could be a place, an item, specific people, etc.)
- Imagine a day in your future living your manifestation. What would the day look like? (The more details, the better!)
- What can you do today to help your manifestation come to life? (Could be affirmations related to the manifestation, related thoughts, beliefs, taking some action/inaction/letting go/taking a step back)
- How can you let go of the "how" and the "when" so that you live in the present moment while allowing your manifestations to step into your life?
- What can you tell your future self when they need that extra push or feel defeated about their manifestation? (You can end the journal entry with a small note to your future self to keep believing so they can read it when things get rough.)

What you are
intentional about
is what is achieved.

I have an abundance of love.	I have an abundance of wealth.	My career is fulfilling.
I am materially abundant.	I have an abundance of family and friends.	I have an abundance of positive emotions.

MANIFESTATION

I am divinely protected.	I am intellectually abundant.	I have an abundance of time.
I have an abundance of physical, mental, emotional and soul health.	I have an abundance of energy.	I have an abundance of creativity.

I have an abundance of gratitude.	I have abundant access to nature.	I have abundant freedom and independence in my life.
I have an abundance of joy in my life.	I have an abundance of self-love and self-acceptance in my life.	I have an abundance of inner peace and calm in my life.

MANIFESTATION

I have an abundance of healthy friendships in my life.	I have an abundance of innovative ideas.	I have an abundance of wisdom.
I have an abundance of experience in my life.	I have an abundance of graciousness and generosity towards others.	I have an abundance of choices.

I have an abundance
of opportunities.

I have an abundance
of growth.

I have an abundance
of good luck.

I have an abundance
of laughter in my life.

I have an abundance
of purpose and meaning
in my life.

I have an abundance
of adventures
in my life.

MANIFESTATION

I have an abundance
of possibilities
in my life.

I have an abundance
of forgiveness towards
myself and others.

I have an abundance
of empathy
and compassion.

I have an abundance
of resilience.

I have an abundance
of wonderment.

I have an abundance
of motivation.

I have an abundance of courage.	I have an abundance of playfulness.	I have an abundance of curiosity.
I have an abundance of belongingness.	I feel safe. I am safe.	I'm in a loving and supportive relationship.

MANIFESTATION

My home is peaceful and harmonious.	I have a successful business.	I have an enjoyable hobby.
I have good leadership skills.	I have good communication skills.	I have good decision-making skills.

I have good
time management
skills.

I have good
organization skills.

I have good focus
and concentration.

I have a good memory
and learning skills.

I have good
public speaking skills.

I have good
negotiation skills.

MANIFESTATION

I have good
persuasion skills.

I have good
conflict resolution
skills.

I have high levels
of self-confidence.

I am constantly
discovering myself.

I have good
problem-solving skills.

I am adaptable.

My body is ___ .	I am good at regulating my emotions.	I have let go of my grudges.
I have good intuition.	I set healthy boundaries.	I cope well with stress.

MANIFESTATION

I embrace change and uncertainty.	I handle constructive criticism and rejection with grace.	I easily let go of what is not meant for me.
I handle success and recognition with humility.	I set and prioritize my goals.	I constantly manifest my dreams and desires.

I take calculated risks and step out of my comfort zone.	I listen actively.	I am a good communicator.
I work well with others.	I inspire and motivate others.	I am a good mentor.

MANIFESTATION

I am a good leader.	I am a good spouse / wife / husband / girlfriend / boyfriend / partner / friend / daughter / son / person.	I accept failure with grace and a healthy mindset.
I appreciate and live in the present moment.	I have achieved my dream of ___ .	I actively practice self-care and self-love.

I trust myself inexplicably.

I have good interpersonal skills.

I make smart financial decisions.

MANIFESTATION

I am self-aware.

I can manage my anxiety effectively.

I have the power to overcome any obstacle that comes my way.

RELATIONSHIPS

Importance:

This part of my self-love journey came a little bit later. The more I got to know myself, the more I realized there were always going to be parts of me that I wouldn't understand just yet—new thoughts, feelings, and actions that would need more time for me to dig deeper. Then the question arose in my mind–If there were parts of myself that I couldn't fully understand yet, how could I expect someone else to understand me on their own?

This was a significant realization because, throughout my life, I had expected people to understand me and intuitively know my needs. I would often be unhappy when they didn't meet my expectations. I don't blame the other person, especially since I hadn't gained clarity about my identity and needs. The minute I realized that it was my responsibility to understand myself and then learn how to communicate my needs to the people around me, my relationships became lighter, and I felt more loved.

This chapter of journal prompts aims to help you get to know yourself better in the context of relationships. Now relationships can mean anything ranging from platonic, romantic, familial, to even work relationships. Then, of course, towards the latter half, the prompts are more centered around your relationship with your partner. Now, if you aren't in a relationship and wish to get into one someday, you can still answer those questions to understand yourself better. For the part of the question about your partner, take the time to analyze your negotiables and non-negotiables. What beliefs, views, and values are you accepting of, and which ones will you not tolerate so on and so forth?

The more clarity you gain on who you are, and as an extension of that, what are your needs and wants for any relationship, I believe the easier it becomes to walk away from people who do not align with you. I learned this the hard way: Relationships are hard work, yes, but they should never be an uphill battle, and the simplest way to find people ready to work with you on the relationship is to start with YOU.

Journal Structure:

Here are some additional questions to help you structure each journal entry after you've picked a prompt to work on:

- What instances or life experiences come to mind that can outline your thoughts even more?
- How can you be more accepting of your needs, wants, and desires?
- How can you remind yourself of your needs, wants, and desires?
- As you evolve, how can you keep getting to know yourself?
- How can you recognize changes in your needs, wants, and desires?

What ties you to you

ties you to everyone else too.

What are some personality traits of ___ that you admire?

What are your personality traits that show up in your relationship with ___ ?

What are the similarities and differences in the way you show up for different relationships in your life? Why is that so?

Write about the different versions of you that exist with every person in your life.

How does ___ perceive you?

What are the strengths you bring in your relationship with ___?

RELATIONSHIPS

What are your weaknesses that show up in your relationship with ___ ?

What are the strengths of ___ that show up in your relationship with them?

What are the weaknesses of ___ that show up in your relationship with them?

How does ___'s family background affect the way they show up in your relationship? *(both positive and negative)*

How does your family background affect the way you show up in your relationship with ___ ?

What are the aspirations of ___ and what is the impact of it on your relationship with them?

What are
the hobbies and
interests of ___
and what is
the impact of it
on your relationship
with them?

What are ___'s
fears and anxieties
about their relationship
with you?

What are
some of the ways
you can be
more understanding
towards ___'s fears
and anxieties?

What are
your fears and anxieties
about your relationship
with ___ ?

What are
some of the ways
___ is understanding
towards your fears
and anxieties?

What are your needs
in your relationship
with ___ ?

RELATIONSHIPS

How do you wish
to be treated in your
romantic relationship?

How do you wish
to be treated
in your friendships?

What is
your list of
non-negotiables
for your relationships?

*(platonic, familial,
romantic, work, etc)*

What are the
good-to-haves
for your relationships?

*(platonic, familial,
romantic, work, etc)*

How does
your past relationships
affect the way
you show up
in your relationship
with ___ ?

How do you
communicate
your thoughts to ___ ?
How can you improve
your communication?

73

How does ___ communicate their thoughts to you? How do you perceive their communication style?

What are some of the ways you can show up with an assertive communication style?

How do you perceive love from everything around you?

(From people, pets, places, the Universe, Higher Power, etc)

How does ___ perceive love?

How can you effectively communicate your love to the people in your life?

What are some of the ways you can cater to the love language of ___ ?

RELATIONSHIPS

What parts of you would you like to improve on so that you can form healthy relationships?

What are your beliefs and values? How do they impact your relationship with ___ ?

What are ___ 's beliefs and values? How do they impact their relationship with you?

What are your spiritual and / or religious views? How do they impact your relationship with ___ ?

What are ___ 's spiritual and / or religious views? How do they impact your relationship with them?

What is your sense of humor like and how does it impact your relationship with ___ ?

What is ___'s sense of humor like and how does it impact your relationship with them?

How would you describe your relationship with yourself? How can you make it better?

How would you describe your relationship with ___?

What are your insecurities and how do they impact your relationship with ___?

What are ___'s insecurities and how do they impact your relationship with them?

How can your loved ones be more mindful of your insecurities? How do you expect people to respond to your insecurities?

RELATIONSHIPS

How do you respond to ___'s insecurities? How can you be more mindful?

Where do your relationship related insecurities stem from?

What do you base your self-worth on and how does that impact your relationships?

What does ___ base their self-worth on and how does it impact their relationship with you?

What are your biggest achievements in your relationship with ___?

What are ___'s biggest achievements in their relationship with you?

What are
your emotional needs
from a
romantic relationship?

What are
your emotional needs
from friendships?

What are
your emotional needs
from your
familial relationships?

What are
your physical needs
from a
romantic relationship?

What are ___'s
emotional needs from
their relationships?

What are
your partner's needs
from a
romantic relationship?

RELATIONSHIPS

What are ___'s
expectations of you?
How does that
make you feel?

What are
the biggest challenges
in your relationship
with ___ ?

What are your thoughts
on having kids?
How does that impact
your relationship
with your partner?

What are
your partner's thoughts
on having kids?
How does that impact
their relationship
with you?

What are your views
on parenting?

What are
your partner's views
on parenting?
How is it similar /
different from yours?

What are
___'s favorite things
about you?

Who are
your role models
for relationships?
How does it impact
the way you show up
for your relationships?

Who are
your partner's
role models
for relationships?
How does it impact
how they show up
for your relationship?

How are your views
on finances and
money management
similar / different
from your partner's?

How are
your views on life
similar / different
from your partner's?

How are
your views on family
similar / different
from your partner's?

RELATIONSHIPS

How are your views
on gender roles
similar / different
from your partner's?

How are your views
on education
and learning
similar / different
from your partner's?

How are your views
on death
similar / different
from your partner's?

How are your views
on success
similar / different
from your partner's?

How are your views
on forgiveness
similar / different
from your partner's?

How are your views
on food and nutrition
similar / different
from your partner's?

How are your views on health and fitness similar / different from your partner's?

How are your views on technology and social media similar / different from your partner's?

How are your views on travel and adventure similar / different from your partner's?

How are your views on self-expression similar / different from your partner's?

How are your views on human rights and social justice issues similar / different from your partner's?

How are your views on marriage and relationships similar / different from your partner's?

RELATIONSHIPS

How are your views on self-care and self-love similar / different from your partner's?

How are your views on sexuality and intimacy similar / different from your partner's?

How are your views about the future similar / different from your partner's?

How are your views on personal growth and development similar / different from your partner's?

How are your views on community service and volunteering similar / different from your partner's?

How are your views on personal style and fashion similar / different from your partner's?

How are your views
on ageing
similar / different
from your partner's?

How are your views
on therapy
and counseling
similar / different
from your partner's?

How are your views
on cultural traditions,
practices, religion,
views on spirituality
similar / different
from your partner's?

RELATIONSHIPS

How are your views
on social relationships
similar / different
from your partner's?

How are your views
on personal boundaries
and privacy
similar / different
from your partner's?

How are your
decision making /
problem solving
methods
similar / different
from your partner's?

ANXIETY

Importance:

Journaling thoughts about my anxiety has been a game-changer for me in managing my anxiety. It's provided a healthy outlet for releasing any pent-up thoughts or feelings that otherwise would have been constantly circling my mind.

I like this practice because it allows me to revisit my thoughts, feelings, and emotions when I'm in a better state of mind. I usually take a different colored pen and write my objective views on the side as I look at the experience from a third person's POV.

It has also helped me find patterns in my thoughts, enabling me to work on unlearning them or reframing them into healthier, more realistic, and balanced thoughts. Writing about my anxiety has also given me a unique opportunity to see my progress. Given how helpless my anxiety makes me feel sometimes, it brings me comfort to see little signs of improvement and makes me more determined to keep going.

Given that I'm putting in the energy to convert my thoughts into writing, it momentarily takes my mind off what I'm experiencing or have experienced and allows me to be in the present moment. I would say that journaling my thoughts, feelings, and experiences about anxiety has been one of the best strategies to work for me. There's something about having your experience written on paper that makes it tangible and not something that's in your head and, in a way, helps to validates one's experience.

In this chapter, I lay out questions to help you understand your anxiety better. If the prompts lead to more tangents, allow it to flow. Given that each person's experiences with anxiety are unique, these prompts should just be a starting point to better understand yourself and your anxiety.

Journal Structure:

Here are some additional questions to help you structure each journal entry after you've picked a prompt to work on:

- What additional information (thoughts, feelings, emotions, actions, past experiences, people who were part of the experience, etc.) would you like to add?
- How can you build long-term systems to protect your well-being as you document your anxiety?
- *When you revisit previous journal entries on your anxiety—* View the journal entry objectively as a third person. What are your thoughts, feelings for the person who has written the entry? What can you say to make them feel better about their experience? How can you validate their experiences? (You can write this in a different color pen.)

Stay proud of your

battle scars.

On a scale of 1-10, how was your anxiety today? How do you feel about it?

Think of a situation you have been in. On a scale of 1-10, how would you rate your anxiety prior to / while experiencing that situation. Why?

Think of a specific person you are around. On a scale of 1-10, how would you rank your anxiety around them? Why?

What are the recurring thoughts that happen in your mind when you are experiencing an anxiety episode?

What are the physical sensations you feel when your anxiety is rising or when you are having an anxiety episode?

What are the emotions you feel when your anxiety is rising or when you are having an anxiety episode?

ANXIETY

In which situations or around which people do you find your anxiety triggered? Why?

How can you avoid your anxiety triggers?

What coping methods have you tried for managing your anxiety? Rank their effectiveness on a scale of 1-10.

How would you describe your anxiety?

What is your reflex reaction to an anxiety episode?

How does your anxiety affect the way you show up in your romantic relationships?

How does your anxiety affect the way you show up in your work relationships?

How does your anxiety affect the way you show up in your platonic friendships?

How does your anxiety affect the way you show up in your familial relationships?

How do your thoughts change when you are experiencing an anxiety episode?

How do you feel about yourself when you are experiencing an anxiety episode?

How do you want to feel about yourself when you are experiencing an anxiety episode?

ANXIETY

How do your beliefs change when you are having an anxiety episode?

How do your actions change when you are experiencing an anxiety episode?

How does your energy change when you are experiencing an anxiety episode?

What is it that you are most afraid of? Why do you think that is?

What previous experiences initiated your anxiety? *(trigger incident)* How do you feel about those experiences today?

If you faced your trigger incident today, how would you react differently?

How can you look at your trigger incident in a healthy way?	As painful as it is to deal with anxiety, try to list the ways your anxiety has actually protected / helped you.	What has your anxiety taught you?
On a scale of 1-10, how much does your anxiety impact your daily life? What steps can you take to reduce it?	On a scale of 1-10, how motivated are you to reduce your anxiety? How can you increase your motivation?	On a scale of 1-10, how confident are you about managing your anxiety? How can you increase your confidence?

ANXIETY

On a scale of 1-10, how hopeful are you about bringing your anxiety under control? How can you increase your hope?	On a scale of 1-10, how comfortable are you talking about your anxiety with your loved ones? Why or why not?	How do you wish for your partner to perceive your anxiety?
How do you wish for your friends to perceive your anxiety?	How do you wish for your family to perceive your anxiety?	How do you want to perceive your anxiety?

What are
some of the actions
your partner can take
to make you
feel supported when
you are experiencing
an anxiety episode?

How comfortable
are you sharing
your needs with
your partner about
your anxiety?
Why or why not?

What are
some of the actions
your friends can take
to make you
feel supported when
you are experiencing
an anxiety episode?

How comfortable
are you to share
your needs
with your friends
about your anxiety?
Why or why not?

What are some actions
your family can take
to make you feel
supported about
your anxiety?

How comfortable
are you to share
your needs with
your family about
your anxiety?
Why or why not?

ANXIETY

What are some actions
people at work can take
to make you
feel supported
about your anxiety?

How comfortable
are you sharing
your needs with
the people at work
about your anxiety?
Why or why not?

Write a letter
to remind yourself
that you are strong and
capable of managing
your anxiety.

Visualize successfully
overcoming
your anxiety.
How would
you show up?
How would that
make you feel?

On a scale of 1-10,
how much shame
do you feel for
having anxiety? Why?

What were
the instances that
triggered shame in you
for experiencing
anxiety?

What are some steps you can take to reduce shame for experiencing anxiety?	Details out the places where you feel calm and relaxed.	Write about some of the strategies you would like to try out to manage your anxiety.
If today was a particularly hard day when your anxiety made you feel helpless, share your thoughts on it.	Imagine yourself without any shame for experiencing anxiety. How would you show up?	Imagine yourself without any guilt for experiencing anxiety. How would you show up?

ANXIETY

Imagine yourself as someone who has learned to manage your anxiety well. How would you show up?	How do you feel when someone understands your anxiety? Detail the incident and the experience.	How do you feel when someone undermines your anxiety? Detail the incident and the experience.
How do you react when someone undermines your anxiety?	How would you like to react when someone undermines your anxiety?	If someone wants to understand more about your anxiety, how would you explain it?

On a scale of 1-10, how open are you to seeking professional help for managing your anxiety? Why or why not?

What are the qualities you seek in a mental health professional?

What are the qualities you do not want in a mental health professional?

What are the physical reactions you have when your anxiety is triggered?

What unhealthy coping mechanisms have you developed because of your anxiety? How can you overcome them / be more cognizant of them?

What physical ailments have developed because of your anxiety? How can you mitigate the damage to your body?

ANXIETY

What affirmations can you tell yourself to help you cope with your anxiety better?

On a scale of 1-10, how detached do you feel from reality? What prompts can you use to be more conscious of your reality?

On a scale of 1-10, how self-aware are you about managing your anxiety? How can you improve on that?

Write a letter to your anxiety. Share how it protected you in times of need. Shower it with love, kindness and compassion.

If this applies, write a letter to the person / people who were the cause for your anxiety.

If this applies, write a letter to someone you wished understood your anxiety, but chose not to.

If this applies, write a letter to someone who took the time to understand your anxiety, showed you love and compassion.

Write a letter to yourself to read when your anxiety is triggered.

On a scale of 1-10, how often do you recognize your triggers? How can you be more aware?

What are some of the steps you can take to avoid your triggers?

What can you tell people so that they can stop inadvertently triggering your anxiety?

On a scale of 1-10, how quickly do you recognize you are having an anxiety episode? How can you help yourself recognize it sooner?

ANXIETY

How long do each of your anxiety episodes last? Describe them.

(slow / fast buildup / one or many thoughts, etc)

On a scale of 1-10, do you avoid dealing with your anxiety? How can you encourage yourself to face it?

How does your anxiety and subsequent behavior changes affect the people around you?

What are some of the ways you can protect the people you love from the negative effects of your anxiety?

Have you hurt the people you love because of your anxiety? How do you feel about it?

If applicable, how can you overcome the guilt of your anxiety hurting the people you love?

On a scale of 1-10, how guilty do you feel for experiencing anxiety? Do you perceive your anxiety to be a burden on your loved ones?

Why do you feel guilty about experiencing anxiety?

What beliefs contribute to your guilt for experiencing anxiety?

ANXIETY

What are the ways that your guilt is hindering you from fully experiencing life / showing up in your relationships?

How can you shift your beliefs so that you don't feel guilty / like a burden for experiencing anxiety?

List 10 things you can visualize doing in the future that your anxiety stops you from doing today.

INNER CHILD
HEALING

Importance:

This is possibly my favorite chapter in the entire book. Honestly, I could cry thinking about the battles my inner child has been through and how wounded she was when I started my healing journey. I have put in so much effort over the years that today, my inner child feels loved and safe to come out and play. It has been very challenging but, at the same time, so liberating, which is why this book is dedicated to my inner child.

As I find deeper aspects of my inner child to heal, I'd like to share how much more beautiful my life has become since I started this journey. Healing my inner child wounds helped me discover my true, authentic self, which gave me the courage to find people who aligned with my authentic self and detach from people I couldn't be myself with. This led to healthier relationships which have made my life more fulfilling.

Healing my inner child also taught me how to embrace vulnerability. I had suppressed my vulnerability for years, believing it was a hindrance. But the more I embraced it, the more I recognized and fell in love with the imperfections within me. It has been such a magical experience that continues to bring me inner peace.

The joy, curiosity, and playfulness in my life have been restored, and I truly believe the ability to look at the world with wonder is a blessing, and I'd have never been able to do so if it weren't for my inner child. I owe a lot of who I am today to her.

This chapter of journal prompts aims to help you get to know your inner child and give them the love they have always deserved from you. The prompts also allow you to reparent yourself and find ways to honor your inner child especially as you move through adulthood. I hope you too, experience how beautiful life becomes when your inner child feels safe and loved.

Journal Structure:

Here are some additional questions to help you structure each journal entry after you've picked a prompt to work on:

- What instances or life experiences come to mind that can outline your thoughts even more?
- How can you allow and honor your inner child's needs, wants, and desires? What steps can you take to allow your inner child to come out and play?
- Based on your prompt, how can you show love toward that aspect of your inner child?
- As life gets tougher, what steps can you take to keep reminding yourself to be kind, patient, and loving towards your inner child in the future?

All your inner child asks for

is your love.

Think back to when
you were a child.
How did you
see yourself
back then?

How do you see
your younger self?

*(Write for every
significant age.)*

What was
the happiest moment
in your childhood?

What was
the saddest moment
in your childhood?

How did you
experience life
as a child?

What were
recurring patterns
of behavior that
you exhibited as a child
to protect yourself?

INNER CHILD HEALING

What made you happy
as a child?

What made you sad
as a child?

What made you scared
as a child?

What made you angry
as a child?

What made you anxious
as a child?

How did you express
your happiness
as a child?

How did you express love as a child?	How did you express your sadness as a child?	How did you express your anger as a child?
How did you express fear as a child?	Make a list of the top 5-10 best memories of your childhood and write about what makes them so memorable to you.	How did you see the world as a child? What was your perception of the world as a child?

INNER CHILD HEALING

How did you see your loved ones *(or a particular person)* as a child?	What kind of a child would you categorize yourself as and why? *(abandoned, playful, cheerful, fearful, guilty, etc)*	How does your inner child perceive love?
What does your inner child consider as a 'safe space'? How can you create it for them?	What were the most prominent feelings you felt as a child and why? *(It would be helpful to mention the situations surrounding those feelings too.)*	What were your struggles as a child?

What were your strengths as a child?	What activities did you enjoy doing as a child?	If you could go back in time and talk to yourself when you were a child, what would you say?
When were the moments you felt least safe as a child?	What were your insecurities as a child? What are your thoughts about it now, as an adult?	Write about the incidents that hurt you when you were a child. How has it affected the way you show up today?

INNER CHILD HEALING

Write about the incidents that made you feel helpless as a child. How has it affected the way you show up today?	Write about the moments you felt neglected as a child. *(Emotional, physical, psychological, etc.)*	What makes your inner child feel seen and heard? Write about how you can make your inner child feel more seen and heard.
What are the thoughts of your inner child right now? How can you honor them with love and compassion?	What actions does your inner child want to take now? How can you honor them with love and compassion?	What kind of people does your inner child feel safe around?

How can you
be more receptive
and supportive of
your inner child?

What can you say
to your inner child
to make them
feel more safe?

How can you be
more sensitive
to the needs of
your inner child?

What coping
mechanisms
did you develop
as a child?
How did
those mechanisms
protect you back then?

What kind of
relationships
did you wish for
as a child?

*(romantic, platonic,
familial, etc)*

How were you
spoken to as a child?
Was it healthy?
If it wasn't,
how can you
reparent yourself now?

INNER CHILD HEALING

How were you
treated as a child?
Was it healthy?
If it wasn't,
how can you
reparent yourself now?

How were you taught
to behave as a child?
Was it healthy?
If it wasn't,
how can you
reparent yourself now?

How were you taught
to express yourself
as a child?
Was it healthy?
If it wasn't,
how can you
reparent yourself now?

How were you taught
to deal with
your emotions
as a child?
Was it healthy?
If it wasn't,
how can you
reparent yourself now?

How were
your actions perceived
when you were a child?
Was it healthy?
If it wasn't,
how can you
reparent yourself now?

How were you taught
right from wrong
as a child?
Was it healthy?
If it wasn't,
how can you
reparent yourself now?

How have the wounds of your inner child affected the way you show up today? How can you reparent yourself?

How have the wounds of your inner child affected your current day relationships? How can you reparent yourself?

How have the wounds of your inner child affected the way you show up for your business / work? How can you reparent yourself?

What triggers your inner child wounds?

(Take time to observe.)

What actions can you take to manage the triggers for your inner child wounds?

What can you tell your inner child to help manage the triggers?

(You can write words of affirmation too!)

INNER CHILD HEALING

What actions can you take to heal your inner child wounds?

What emotions do you feel when your inner child is triggered? How can you be kind to yourself when you are triggered?

What steps can you take to protect your inner child?

How can you forgive the people who have hurt your inner child?

(Even if they don't apologize.)

What can you do to forgive yourself for neglecting your inner child?

What can you do to remind yourself to care for your inner child?

Write a letter to yourself from the perspective of your inner child.	If you could recreate one memory from your childhood, what would it be? Can you actually recreate parts of it *(or the entire thing)* today?	What were hurtful things that were said to you when you were a child? How can you change your perception about it today?
Imagine you are a child again. What would a perfect day in your life look like? How can you recreate that as an adult?	Imagine you are a child again. What would you like to see, think, feel, and experience? How can you recreate that as an adult?	Imagine you are a child again. What would you like to have that was missing before? How can you give that to yourself as an adult?

INNER CHILD HEALING

Remember how you were as a child. What were your best qualities?	Remember how you were as a child. Write about the way you were doing your best, given the circumstances.	Reaffirm to your inner child about how much you love them unconditionally.
Reaffirm to your inner child that it was okay to have dealt with the situation(s) with what they knew best at the time.	Reaffirm to your inner child about why they shouldn't feel any guilt or shame.	Reaffirm to your inner child about the growth that you have had so far.

Write about
your progress so far
with your
inner child healing.

What has changed
in your perception
when you look back
at your childhood?

What kind of
environment
can you
consciously create
so that your
inner child is happy?

What kind of
environment
must you avoid
so that your inner child
can feel safe
and happy?

Write down
a list of affirmations
to comfort your
inner child.

Remind yourself
of the knowledge
and resources
you have now,
that you did not
as a child.

INNER CHILD HEALING

How can you show
your inner child
more acceptance?

Write about
the situations
where you were brave
as a child.

Write about
the situations where
you were forced to
grow up. How would
you reparent yourself
today? How can you
create the experiences
you missed as a child?

What makes
the innocence
of your inner child
so pure?
How can you
embody that today?

What would your
5 / 10 / 15 year old self
say to you
when they look
at you today?

*(You can choose
a specific age too.)*

What were
some of the things
you were scared to say /
do / feel when you were
a child? After writing,
respond to it with
your thoughts as
your current self.

Ask your inner child
to describe
their childhood
in one word and
you do the same too.
Why and how are they
different / similar?

What were you
not given as a child
that you wish to
provide for your
child / children?

What were you given
as a child that
you wish to provide for
your child / children?

INNER CHILD HEALING

Visualize
a version of you
with a healed
inner child.
Describe how you
would think / act and
see / feel /
experience life.

Visualize having
a conversation with
a healed inner child
version of
your future self.
What do you see?
What would you
say to them?

Visualize handling
an inner child trigger
in a healthy way.
How do you respond?
What actions
do you take? What are
your thoughts?
How did it feel?

TRAUMA
HEALING

Importance:

One of the things that I struggled with, and frankly, took me two whole years of journaling, was calling some of my life experiences for what they truly were–Trauma.

For one, I kept minimizing the effects of my traumas because I didn't want to be pitied or thought of as a victim. Other people were involved in some of my traumas, and I was afraid it would cause more problems if I recognized those incidents as trauma. I kept pushing those experiences as "part of life," and it blew up in my face. I started to observe my trauma responses seeping into some of my business decisions, and it was clear that I was making a mistake. That was a wake-up call for me to learn how to acknowledge the trauma I had been through and, second, its continued impact on all areas of my life.

I couldn't have done it without journaling. And that is what the chapter aims at. Some of the prompts are from my vault. They have helped me create a safe space to heal, recognize my trauma, acknowledge it, process what exactly happened, validate my experiences, face the complex emotions that come with it, create emotional distance between me and the trauma so that I can rewrite the narrative in a way that empowers me, give me a sense of control over my life today, remove self-blame, slowly release the weight that I've been carrying for a long, long, long time in my life, identifying my triggers so that I can manage and avoid retraumatization, create systems to help me manage the effects of it, and last but not least, taught me that I deserve peace in my life despite everything I have been through. I'm still in my healing journey, and of course, it is a lifelong process, but this is where my prompts have led me thus far. I hope these prompts help you feel seen and validate the trauma you have been through. It is a battle; to fight for every inch of peace, but I hope you will find the effort worth it, just as I have.

If at any point, you find yourself distressed, please seek professional help.

Journal Structure:

Here are some additional questions to help you structure each journal entry after you've picked a prompt to work on:

- What specific instances or life experiences come to mind that came later in your life but connects back to the prompt?
- What are you feeling right now, as you are working through the prompt? What thoughts, emotions, feelings are coming up? Document that as well.
- What are some steps you can take to feel better after an intense journaling session?
- What are some kind words you can write for your future self when you look back at these journal entries?

The most healing thing

you can do for yourself

is to honor your story.

What do you define as trauma?	On a scale of 1-10, how comfortable are you to acknowledge your experience as trauma? Why or why not?	On a scale of 1-10, how difficult is it for you to recognize trauma in your life? Why is that so?
Narrate the traumatic incident(s) from a third person's perspective. What do you see / feel / think?	Narrate the traumatic incident(s) from your perspective - What was the sequence of events?	Narrate the traumatic incident(s) from your perspective - What were your feelings at every instance?

TRAUMA HEALING

Narrate the traumatic incident(s) from your perspective - What were your thoughts at every instance?	Narrate the traumatic incident(s) from your perspective - What were your actions at every instance?	Narrate the traumatic incident(s) from your perspective - Were there any people around? What did they do? How did they react?
Are there any parts of your experience that are too painful to talk about? If yes, name each of those experiences with a word that you love.	(Continued) After choosing a word you love, keep adding one sentence to it whenever you feel ready.	What recurring thoughts do you have about your trauma? How do those thoughts make you feel?

On a scale of 1-10, how worried are you that you might be exaggerating your trauma in your mind? What can you do to honor your trauma?

How do you feel about the place / situation / people who caused your trauma?

Write a letter to the people who caused your trauma. What would you say to them? *(You don't have to send the letter.)*

Write a letter to your younger self when they were experiencing the trauma - What kind words would you like to share with them?

Write a letter to your younger self when they were experiencing the trauma - What did you wish someone had told them?

Write a letter to your younger self when they were experiencing the trauma - What do you wish they knew about the future?

TRAUMA HEALING

On a scale of 1-10, how guilty do you feel when you want to hold people accountable for your trauma? How can you be kind to yourself as you feel this way?

How can you set boundaries with people as you heal from your trauma?

How can you set boundaries with people who are inducing trauma to you?

How can you show compassion towards yourself as you heal from trauma?

Write 10 self-affirmations to read every day as you heal from your trauma.

How does your past trauma impact the way you show up today in your professional life?

How does your past trauma impact the way you show up today in your platonic relationships?

How does your past trauma impact the way you show up today in your romantic relationships?

How does your past trauma impact the way you show up today in your familial relationships?

How do you feel when you find your past trauma impacting your life today?

What are the recurring thoughts you have when you find your past trauma impacting your life today?

What kind words can you say to yourself when you find your past trauma impacting your life today?

TRAUMA HEALING

What recurring thoughts about your past trauma do you have that are objectively not true? How can you reframe those thoughts?

If your past trauma repeated itself today, how would you react to it? How would you handle it differently?

Compare the person you were when your trauma happened to the person you are today. How have you grown as a person?

What fears has your past trauma brought up in your present day life?

What unhealthy coping mechanisms did you develop from your past trauma? How can you replace them with healthy coping mechanisms?

How can you rebuild trust within yourself as you continue to heal?

How do you feel about your trauma healing process?	What can your loved ones do to support you in your trauma healing journey?	What have been the psychological, emotional and physical impact of your trauma? How can you hold space for it?
What scares you most about your past trauma?	On a scale of 1-10, how guilty do you feel about your trauma and its impact on the people in your life? Why do you feel that way?	How can you develop a healthy perspective on the impact of your trauma on other people in your life?

TRAUMA HEALING

On a scale of 1-10, do you water down your trauma so that people around you will be more comfortable? How can you honor your trauma better?	On a scale of 1-10, how difficult do you think it is for someone to accommodate your triggers? What is the objective truth?	On a scale of 1-10, do you think your past trauma is a burden on the people you love? What is the objective truth?
How can you communicate your triggers to your loved ones?	How has your past trauma affected your body?	What are the physical reactions that you have when you face a trigger?

What are the emotional reactions you have when you face a trigger?	What are the thoughts you have when you face a trigger?	Write 10 self-affirmations to repeat to yourself when you are facing a trigger.
What do you do if someone unknowingly triggers you? How can you respond in a healthy way?	What do you do if someone intentionally triggers you? How can you respond in a healthy way?	What would you like to do if someone does not respect your triggers?

TRAUMA HEALING

Have there been any significant changes to your personality because of your past trauma? How do you feel about it?	How can you learn to love the 'new you' post trauma?	How can you honor and let go of the person you were before you experienced the trauma?
How can you show love and kindness towards the person you were forced to become during the trauma?	How can you be kind towards the decisions you made while you were experiencing trauma?	How can you be kind to yourself when you have sudden outbursts?

How can you be kind to yourself as you learn to regulate your emotions?	Have you been having flashbacks? Can you try describing them? How are you feeling about it? How would you like to feel about it?	Have you been having nightmares about your past trauma? What steps can you take to make yourself feel comforted when you wake up?
How can you process and perceive your flashbacks / nightmares in a healthy way?	How can you be kind to yourself when you feel frustrated about the lack of control over your reactions because of your past trauma?	On a scale of 1-10, how guilty do you feel about bringing a partner into a life you have spent healing from? How can you have a healthier perspective on it?

TRAUMA HEALING

How can you protect yourself from ongoing trauma? *(complex trauma)*	How can you avoid triggers from ongoing trauma?	How can you create a safe environment for yourself when you are going through trauma? *(complex trauma)*
On a scale of 1-10, do you feel weak and helpless about your past trauma? How can you have a healthier perspective?	On a scale of 1-10, do you feel weak and helpless about your ongoing trauma *(complex trauma)*? How can you honor your truth?	Write about your ongoing trauma experiences from a third person's perspective. *(Repeat this as many times as you would like & notice the changes in your narrative over time.)*

How can you learn to trust situations / people around you after trauma?	What steps can you take to trust your loved ones better after the trauma?	What steps can you take to connect with people in a healthy way after the trauma?
What steps can you take to build a safe space for yourself after the trauma?	What are some of the healthy ways that you can lean on your loved ones for support? How can you communicate it to them?	How can you deal with the emotions associated with people who caused the trauma? Which way honors the trauma while being healthy?

TRAUMA HEALING

What steps can you add to your daily routine to help you be more kind and mindful of your past trauma?	What are some steps you can take to let go of resentment towards your trauma?	How can you be more accepting that your trauma is a part of your past?
As difficult as it may be, list some of the positives that came from your trauma. *(It's okay if there was none.)*	What are the steps you can take to avoid passing the trauma onto the people around you? *(spouse, kids, friends, etc)*	Write a letter to your future self about where you are at right now on your healing journey.

Write a letter to your past self about how far you've come in your healing journey. Offer support and encouragement to your past self.

On a scale of 1-10, how safe do you feel to ask for help? How can you make yourself feel more comfortable to ask for help?

Imagine a more healed version of you. What would they think / feel / see / do? What are some of the steps you can take to get there?

TRAUMA HEALING

What thoughts / feelings do you have when you think of a future post your trauma?

What beliefs of yours contribute to healing the trauma?

Have your dreams and aspirations changed post trauma? How so? How do you feel about it? How can you be more accepting of it?

SHADOW WORK

Importance:

I should start with what shadow work means to me. We all have some parts of ourselves that we have repressed. We also have parts of us that occasionally resort to unhealthy, negative, or harmful beliefs, thoughts, coping mechanisms, feelings, actions, etc.

To me, shadow work is about digging into those depths. It is about answering the question, "Why are you, YOU?"

I believe shadow work is about taking everything within you that you perceive isn't pretty and learning to find beauty in who you are as you heal. To me, shadow work is a delicate balance between self-acceptance and self-transcendence. And if you can master that, if you can be comfortable enough to dive within those deep waters and find peace while you transform, you become more conscious of the decisions you are making for your life. An intentional life is a life that is aligned with your authentic self.

In this chapter, you'll find prompts to help you understand where your negative / unhealthy parts come from and how you can heal those parts of you. It also touches upon aspects of you that you may have subconsciously repressed over the years and encourages you to slowly accept them while learning to be proud of your authentic self.

As you work through some shadows, you'll find more coming to the surface and that may overwhelm you sometimes. I hope you can remember that we're only human. We were not built to be perfect. As long as there is continued intention towards evolving into better versions of yourself, I'd say you are doing amazing!!

Journal Structure:

Here are some additional questions to help you structure each journal entry after you've picked a prompt to work on:

- Are there any more shadows coming up as you work through this prompt? What are your thoughts / feelings about it?
- How has this shadow affected other areas of your life? What instances / past experiences are coming to your mind? How do you feel about it?
- How can you remind yourself of the positives of shadow work if / when your future self is struggling to continue?
- How can you create a supportive and kind environment for yourself as you work through your shadows?
- What messages would you like to leave for your future self reviewing your entries?
- How can you recognize the progress you have made? What milestones can you give yourself? How can you celebrate your progress?

Look inwards

to feel lighter.

Think of a situation or a person you feel resentful towards. What part of the experience made you feel wronged?

(Continued) How can you replace your resentment with gratitude?

(For the situation, for the person, etc)

On a scale of 1-10, how long do you hold a grudge? How can you motivate yourself to let go of the grudge?

On a scale of 1-10, how critical are you of yourself? Why do you think that is so?

(Continued) What are the critical thoughts that you have about yourself? How can you let yourself know when your self-criticism is unhealthy?

On a scale of 1-10, how important is control for you?

(Control over situations, people, etc)

SHADOW WORK

How do you think your need for control affects the people around you?

Has your need for control impacted your relationships negatively? How so?

What is your motivation behind working to let go of your unhealthy need for control?

What are a few things you can say to yourself when you find yourself wanting unhealthy control?

How do you feel about your body? What are some of the thoughts that come to your mind when you think about your body?

How can you cultivate a healthier relationship with your body? What can you do to feel better about your body?

Write a letter to your body, outlining all the helpful things it does for you, and all the amazing things it accomplishes.

How do you think others perceive your body? What are the steps you can take to let go of their perception of your body?

What are some of the things that contribute to your self-worth? How can you make your self-worth independent of them?

How does social media affect the way you perceive yourself? How can you detach from that and create a healthy view of yourself?

What significant mistakes have you made that changed the way you view yourself?

What are the different roles you play in your life, and how do you perceive yourself in those roles?

SHADOW WORK

How have your failures changed the way you perceive yourself? How can you change the narrative into a healthier one?

How has your self-perception evolved over time?

(Think about how you perceived yourself at different ages / milestones.)

What triggers your imposter syndrome? What are some of the steps you can take to question the validity of those feelings?

Which situations make you feel unworthy or inadequate? What triggers those feelings? How can you help yourself feel worthy and adequate?

Which previous experiences led to your current feelings of unworthiness and inadequacy? What are your current thoughts on it?

On a scale of 1-10, how hard is it for you to embrace emotional intimacy with someone? Why do you think that is? How do you feel about it?

Why do you think you avoid emotional intimacy? What past experiences led to your fear of intimacy?

What are the thoughts that occur when someone wants to build emotional intimacy with you? How do you feel?

How can you reframe your past experiences to help you be more open to emotional intimacy today?

How has your avoidance of emotional intimacy affected your relationships?

(past / current / familial / platonic / romantic, etc)

What is motivating you to work on overcoming your avoidance for emotional intimacy? How can you keep that motivation going?

What defense mechanisms have you developed to shut yourself off from emotional intimacy? What steps can you take to redirect those actions?

SHADOW WORK

What do you need from your loved ones as you work on your emotional intimacy avoidance? How can they help you better?

Imagine a version of you that is open to emotional intimacy. How would you behave? How would you feel? How would you treat your loved ones?

How can you balance your personal boundaries so that you are not shutting people out while protecting yourself?

On a scale of 1-10, how difficult is it for you to ask for help? Why do you think that is?

What are the thoughts you have when you need help but are unable to ask for it? How can you reframe those thoughts?

How can you make yourself more open to receiving love?

What are
some of the actions
your partner can take
to make you
feel supported
when you are not
your best self?

How comfortable
are you to share
your shortcomings
with your partner?
Why or why not?

What are
some of the actions
your friends can take
to make you
feel supported
when you are not
your best self?

What are you
procrastinating
right now? What fear
is holding you back
from doing the task
at hand?

How do you feel
when you
procrastinate?
How can you be kind
and understanding
towards yourself?

What would you
miss out on
if you continued to
procrastinate?
What would the future
look like? How can you
avoid that future?

SHADOW WORK

How do you feel about
change? Why do you
feel that way?

How do you cope
with change?
How do you feel
about your coping
mechanisms towards
change? How can you
make it better?

Which past
experiences
are you still
holding onto?
How can you
slowly let go of
its influence
and impact on you?

Where does your need
to people-please
come from?
How do you feel
about it?

What do you think
will be the outcome
if you don't
people-please?
How can you change
that narrative into
a healthier one?

Imagine a version
of you that does not
people-please.
A version of you
that lives a life true
to yourself. What
would that look like?
How would you feel?

What stops you from expressing your love freely? Which experiences led to your restraint and hesitance?

What small steps can you take to express your love to your loved ones? How can you let them know *(in your own way)* that they are loved by you?

How often do you judge others? *(For their appearance, decisions, values, etc)* Where do you think that stems from?

Write about a past experience where you misjudged someone. How did that make you feel? What did that teach you?

What steps can you take to be more open and accepting of others around you?

How often do you ask yourself if your needs are being met? How can you be more conscious of it?

SHADOW WORK

Why do you neglect your needs and desires? Where do you think that stems from? How can you reframe that thought process?

What steps can you take to make sure you are consistently meeting your needs and desires?

On a scale of 1-10, how difficult is it for you to accept a compliment? Why do you think that is?

How do you react when someone compliments you? Do you accept it or deflect it? How can you shift your response to acceptance?

What are some steps you can take to remind yourself that you are worthy and deserving of the compliments?

Imagine a version of you that has unleashed their full potential. What would that look like? What's stopping you today?

How often do you find yourself avoiding conflict? What stops you from confrontation? Why do you think that is?

How does your avoidance of conflict make you feel? What are the long-term negative effects of it?

What communication skills can you work on to help you feel confident to embrace conflicts? What other steps can you take?

On a scale of 1-10, how considerate are you of other people's boundaries? How can you be more aware?

What do you need to help yourself feel safe enough to express your vulnerability? How can you communicate that to your loved ones?

What past experiences have made you hesitant to take responsibility for your actions? How can you reframe that to a healthier thought process?

SHADOW WORK

Why do you hesitate to try new experiences? How can you make yourself more open to new experiences?

Write about a past experience when you did not stand up for yourself. How did that make you feel? What would you do differently today?

What does being assertive look like to you? How can you be more assertive in your everyday life?

What past experiences led you to disconnect from your cultural / ancestral heritage? How can you get more in touch with it today?

On a scale 1-10, how difficult is it for you to accept your imperfections? Why do you think that is?

What steps can you take to make yourself feel safe enough to apologize to your loved ones when you make a mistake?

List some of the societal conditioning that hinders the way you show up today. How can you reframe that?

On a scale of 1-10, how difficult is it for you to prioritize your physical well-being? Why do you think that is? How can you prioritize better?

On a scale of 1-10, how difficult is it for you to work on your limiting beliefs? Why do you think that is? How can you make it better?

On a scale of 1-10, how difficult is it for you to embrace inner exploration? Why do you think that is? How can you make it better?

Write about a few childhood friendships that have impacted your adulthood.

(positive / negative)

Are there any cultural prejudices / stereotypes / biases that you knowingly / unknowingly participate in? How can you reduce that?

SHADOW WORK

How has your family dynamics affected your personal growth? How does that make you feel? Is there something you'd like to reframe / work on?

Are there any subconscious beliefs that are hindering you from living your best life? How can you reframe those?

Write a letter to yourself about the significance of your value.

(Value in your thoughts, actions, beliefs, etc. Really hype yourself up!!)

What societal norms have shaped your personal identity? How do you feel about it?

On a scale of 1-10, how difficult is it for you to accept the consequences of your actions? Why do you think that is? How can you make it better?

List all your hidden desires. Why are they hidden? What would make you feel safe to express them?

Write a letter
to yourself about
the person
you are today.

*(Good, bad, ugly, positives,
negatives, everything)*

Write a letter
to yourself outlining
the truth of your
experience in your
healing journey.

Write a letter
to yourself about
all the things you are
ashamed to say out
loud. How can you
create a safe space for
yourself to say
those aloud?

SHADOW WORK

What are your thoughts
on mortality?
How does that
influence your actions
today? How can you
have a healthier
perspective on
mortality?

How easy / difficult is it
for you to embrace
aging? How can you
reframe your mindset
to be more accepting of
the natural process
of life?

How can you show up
better for yourself?

EMOTION
MANAGEMENT

Importance:

This chapter is more about learning where each emotion stems from and what you can do to respond rather than react. It's not about invalidating these emotions; rather, it is about accepting that they are part of us and that we can learn to manage them in a healthy way.

Journal Structure for All:

Here are some additional questions to help you structure each journal entry after you've picked a prompt to work on:

- What are you feeling right now as you are writing the journal entry?
- What instances or life experiences come to mind that can outline your thoughts even more?
- How can you be more accepting of the emotion you are feeling right now?
- How do you feel about the emotion you are writing about?
- What are the recurring thoughts you have when you are experiencing this emotion? How do you feel about it?
- As you evolve, how can you keep getting to know yourself?
- How can you cope with varying degrees of feeling the emotion you are writing about?

Journal Structure for Fear (Page 153):

So, for this particular emotion, I've given a list of fears that one may possibly have. You can pick one fear and write about it. Of course, feel free to create a journal entry with your own personal fears that may not be mentioned. Here are some additional questions to help you structure each journal entry after you've picked a fear to work on:

- What do you hope to achieve with this journal entry about this fear? Do you want to learn how to accept it, or do you want to work on it? Give reasons.
- When was the first time you felt that fear? Detail out the experience. What are your thoughts on the incident today?
- Where do you think this fear stems from? Mention the triggering incident and / or influences if possible.
- How has this fear impacted your life? How do you feel about it? Mention instances.
- How do people react to your fear? How would you like other people to respond to this fear of yours?
- Why do you want to overcome this fear? What motivates you to work on this fear?
- What would a life without this fear look like? How do you feel about it?
- How can you be more accepting of your fear as you work through it?

To regulate emotions is to
first give them permission
to flow.

On a scale of 1-10, how difficult is it for you to recognize your emotions? Why do you think that is?

What are some of the physical reactions you have that you can associate with individual emotions?

On a scale of 1-10, how deeply do you feel emotions? What about other people's emotions? Why do you think that is? How do you feel about it?

What has each emotion you have ever experienced taught you?

What do you define as emotion regulation? How can you help yourself to regulate your emotions better?

EMOTIONS

List a few sentences you can tell yourself during emotionally charged situations to help you respond instead of react.

(When dealing with intense / negative situations)

How can you focus your energy to positive and neutral aspects of your life?

How can you give space for your emotions to be? What can you do to make yourself safe to feel your emotions?

According to you, what constitutes as a healthy expression of emotions? How can you embody that more?

How can you give yourself the space to experience ALL your emotions without feeling overwhelmed?

What does happiness mean to you? When would you say you are in a state of happiness?

What are the elements / factors that contribute to your happiness? What impacts your happiness? Why or how do they do so?

How can you align your belief / values / mindset to bring you more happiness?

What are your struggles with your happiness? Why do you think that is? What steps can you take to reduce your struggle?

How do you express your happiness? What thoughts do you have? What physical reactions do you have?

How would you categorize your relatonship with happiness - Healthy / unhealthy? Why do you feel so?

HAPPINESS

Which elements / factors negatively impacts your happiness? Why do you think that is? How can you protect yourself better?

What parts of your life are directly correlated to your state of happiness? Why do you think that is? How do you feel about it?

Has happiness ever felt forced? Describe the experience. Why did you feel that way? How can you make your happiness more natural and aligned?

How do you feel when someone is happy? Why do you feel that way?

(Name the person, friend, frenemy, family member, etc)

What has life taught you about happiness?

What have the people in your life taught you about happiness?

How authentic
do you feel about
your state of happiness?
How can you be
more authentic
to your experience?

How can you
enhance your potential
for happiness with
habits and routines?

*(For when you feel
happiness)*
Describe every
single thing you are
feeling right now.
How can you
cherish it better?

HAPPINESS

Do you fear happiness?
Why do you think
that is?
What experiences led to
this thought? How can
you reframe that?

What are
some of the steps
you can take to
recognize happiness?
How can you be more
intentional about
happiness?

How can you share
your happiness in a way
that feels authentic
to you?

What do you define as shame? What are the feelings you associate with shame?

What are the physical reactions you have when you feel shame? What are the thoughts? What other emotions do you feel?

Write about an experience when you felt shame. What was your takeaway from the incident? How can you reframe that into a healthier mindset today?

What triggers your shame? Where did they come from?

(List as many as you can.)

How has shame affected your thoughts, behaviors and actions?

How has shame affected your relationships?

(Familial, romantic, platonic, work, etc)

SHAME

How can you reframe your thoughts related to shame?

Has your shame led you to hide parts of yourself? Why do you think that is? How do you feel about it?

(Continued) What are the first few steps you can take to heal the shame and create a safe space for those parts of yourself?

How has shame affected your ability to make decisions for your life? How do you feel about it? What would you like to do about it?

What has shame taken away from you? How can you bring it back?

(It's never too late to reclaim!)

What recurring situations do you find yourself feeling shame? How can you break that cycle?

How has shame impacted your self-esteem and self-worth? Write 10 affirmations to remind yourself of your value and worth.

Has anyone caused feelings of shame within you? *(Unintentionally / intentionally)* How did that make you feel? How do you feel about it now?

(Continued) How can you release the hold of that person / incident on you, and take steps to heal your feelings of shame?

SHAME

Write a letter to yourself coming from a place of kindness and compassion about your feelings of shame.

Imagine leading a life with little / no shame. Just unapologetically being you. How would that look like? What steps can you take today?

Write a letter to console your past self when you felt shame.

How do you define sadness? How do you recognize sadness? What are your individualistic signs?	How do you distinguish sadness from other feelings?	What are the physical reactions you have when you feel sadness? What are the thoughts? What other emotions do you feel?
What triggers your sadness? How can you handle those triggers better?	How does sadness affect your thoughts, beliefs, values, behavior and actions?	Do you feel resentful towards sadness? Why do you think that is? How can you accept sadness in a healthy way?

SADNESS

Write about an experience that brought sadness to you. Why did it make you feel the way it did? How did you start to feel better?	How does sadness affect the way you show up in relationships? *(Familial, platonic, romantic, work, etc)*	How does sadness affect other areas of your life? How do you feel about it?
What are your current coping mechanisms for sadness? How can you improve them?	What are some habits and routines you can add to your life to help you cope with sadness?	How can you hold space for your sadness? How can you be more kind and compassionate to yourself as you navigate your feelings?

How would you like your loved ones to support you when you are sad? How can you communicate it to them?

How can you support yourself as you navigate inevitable situations that bring you sadness?

How can you recognize and remove yourself from avoidable situations that bring you sadness?

SADNESS

How will you know it is time to actively heal? How can you recognize the difference between wallowing in self-pity and holding space for your sadness?

What steps can you take to be more accepting that sadness is a part of the cycle of life? How can you have a healthier relationship with sadness?

Write a letter to your past self when they were experiencing sadness. Fill the letter with everything you wished you were told at the time.

What does guilt mean to you? Where do you think guilt comes from?

What are the thoughts, actions, physical reactions and responses you have when you feel guilt?

What triggers you to feel guilt? How do you distinguish between healthy guilt and unhealthy guilt?

Write about an experience when you felt guilt even though you didn't do anything wrong. Why did it happen? How can you reframe your mindset?

How does healthy guilt impact the way you see yourself? How can you be kind to yourself as you experience healthy guilt?

How does unhealthy guilt impact the way you see yourself? How can you be kind to yourself as you experience unhealthy guilt?

GUILT

Write about an experience when you felt guilt because you did someone wrong. How did you empathize with the other? How can you take responsibility?

How can you convey your healthy guilt to the other person? What would you say / do?

How has unhealthy guilt affected your decision making process? How can you reframe that mindset?

How has guilt affected your interpersonal relationships? *(Healthy / unhealthy guilt)* How do you feel about it?

Describe situations / experiences where societal / cultural norms have made you experience unhealthy guilt. How can you reframe that mindset?

On a scale of 1-10, how severely do you punish yourself when you feel guilt? Why? How can you have a healthier relationship with guilt?

On a scale of 1-10, how scared do you feel about repeating past mistakes because of the guilt you feel? Why? What steps can you take to be more confident?

How can you use healthy guilt to motivate you to become a better version of yourself? How can you be compassionate to yourself as you evolve?

What life lessons has healthy guilt taught you?

GUILT

What life lessons did you learn when you healed unhealthy guilt?

Write a letter to a past version of yourself when you experienced unhealthy guilt. What advice / words of comfort would you give?

Imagine a future where you do not experience any unhealthy guilt. What would that look like?

What do you define as fear? When was the first time you remember experiencing fear? How has that shaped your current feelings about fear?	Write about an experience when you felt most fear. What were the repercussions? How do you feel about the incident today?	How has fear affected the way you show up for your relationships? How does that make you feel? What steps can you take to heal the fear?
What are the positive things about fear? How has fear protected you?	How can you distinguish between healthy and unhealthy fear? How can you foster a healthy relationship with fear?	How has fear impacted your values, beliefs, thoughts? How can you reframe those?

FEAR

How can you embrace fear instead of resisting it? How can you allow fear to exist, but not stop you from living your full life?	Do you hold any resentment for your past self for allowing fear to win? How can you let go of the resentment and forgive your past self?	Imagine a future version of you without a particular fear that you wish to remove. What does that look like? How does it feel?

Read "Journal Structure for Fear" guidelines (Page 140) for these journal prompts.

Fear of Facing Past Trauma Fear of Repeating Unhealthy Family Patterns	Fear of Being Seen as Weak Fear of Feeling Too Much Fear of Acknowledging Negative Personality Traits	Fear of Losing Financial Security Fear of Losing Creativity Fear of Losing Loved Ones
Fear of Failure Fear of Success Fear of Rejection Fear of Being Exposed as a Fraud	Fear of Abandonment Fear of Intimacy Fear of Commitment Fear of Vulnerability Fear of Emotions Fear of Healthy Sexuality	Fear of Letting Go Fear of Change Fear of Making Mistakes Fear of the Unknown Fear of Losing Control of Life

FEAR

Fear of Not Being Loved Fear of Being Unlovable Fear of Not Being Needed Fear of Being Invisible	Fear of Conflict Fear of Being Judged Fear of Consequences	Fear of Being Powerless Fear of Aging Fear of Death Fear of Being Superior Fear of Being Inferior

What does disappointment mean to you?

What are your physical reactions, thoughts, responses when you feel disappointed?

How do you deal with the hopes that have not been met when you are disappointed? How would you like to deal with it?

How do you react when your expectations are not met? How do you react when people don't meet your expectations? Is it a healthy response?

How do you react when a situation is not as good as you had hoped? What are the thoughts you experience?

How do you react when something you hoped for, does not happen? What other feelings do you experience?

DISAPPOINTMENT

Write about a past experience where you were disappointed. What were your initial thoughts about the situation? How do you feel about it today?

How can you keep a positive attitude when you are disappointed? What affirmations can you tell yourself?

How has previous disappointments affected your interpersonal relationships?

How has previous disappointments affected your beliefs, values, attitude towards life? How can you make it healthier?

How has previous disappointments affected your ability to hope? How do you feel about it?

How do you react when you feel disappointed in yourself? How can you be kind to yourself as you navigate through your feelings of disappointment?

How can you adjust your expectations in a healthy way so that you can reduce your chances of being disappointed?

How can you work from where you are at right now, rather than where you hoped to be?

What life lessons have your previous disappointments taught you?

(List as many as possible.)

DISAPPOINTMENT

Are there any other steps you can take to help you reduce the chances of being disappointed?

Write a letter to your past self when they experienced a big disappointment. Share words of consolation and a positive perspective on the situation.

How can you reduce your resentment on people when they disappoint you? How can you be kind to them if they fail to meet your expectations / hopes?

What is the underlying cause for your anger?

(pain, frustration, fear helplessness, guilt, grief, shame, insecurity, etc)

List out situations / actions of people that trigger your anger. Why does it trigger you?

(Continued) What past experiences are tied to your current anger or have led to these triggers? Describe them in detail.

(Continued) What is your anger protecting you from? How can you create a safe space for that part of you?

How do you express your anger? How do you feel about your reaction / response? How do others feel about your reaction / response?

How can you express your anger in a way that is clear, specific yet compassionate?

ANGER

How can you forgive yourself for your past responses to anger that were not healthy for you? What would you do differently today? How have you evolved?

Write few affirmations to remind yourself when you experience anger. How can you keep reminding yourself for it?

How has healthy anger protected you in the past? How can you continue to honor healthy anger?

What can you do to help yourself to pause and consider other perspectives when you are angry?

(For any situation) What are the consequences of unhealthy anger? How do you feel about it? How can you prevent it?

(For any situation) What are the consequences of healthy anger? How do you feel about it? How can you facilitate it?

What are your physical responses to anger? What physical sensations do you feel in your body? How can you understand and manage it?

Do you have any anger harboring against yourself / your past self? Why? How can you heal and send love to yourself?

How has unhealthy anger affected your life? *(work, relationships, personal growth, etc)* How do you feel about it? How do you want to change it?

ANGER

Imagine someone is angry with you. How would you like them to express their anger? How can you be that person to someone else?

Write a letter to someone you are angry with. How can you communicate your thoughts / feelings in a way that honors what you feel while being compassionate?

Write a letter to yourself honoring the protection that healthy anger gives you and healing the negativity that unhealthy anger brings you.

Write a letter to your past self. *(You can choose to write different letters for different stages of your life.)*	Write a letter to your present self, from your inner child.	Write a letter to your present self as the person you are today.
Write a letter to your future self about forgiving any future actions that may not be in alignment.	Write a letter to your inner critic.	Write a letter to the person who was responsible for your complex trauma.

FORGIVENESS

Write a letter to the person who could never admit they were wrong.	Write a letter to the people who misunderstood you.	Write a letter to the people who mistreated you.
Write a letter to the person who could not be there for you in the way you needed them to.	Write a letter to the person who apologized to you, but you were not ready to accept their apology at the time.	Write a letter to a family member.

Write a letter
to someone
who wronged you
when you were a child.

Write a letter
to someone
whose actions had a
significant negative
impact on your life.

Write a letter to an ex,
ex-friend, ex-best
friend, bullies,
adversaries, authority
figures, etc.

FORGIVENESS

Write a letter
to a stranger who
mistreated you.

Write a letter
to someone
you wish to forgive
but has passed away.

Write a letter to society.

(*You can write about how
you choose to forgive, even
though you do not align
with the thoughts, etc*)

What does jealousy mean to you? Why do you think jealousy arises?

What are the reactions, responses, thoughts, feelings that come when you feel jealous?

How do you recognize jealousy within you? What are some of the signs to help you recognize?

When was the first time you remember experiencing jealousy? How do you view the experience today?

How do you interact / behave with someone when you are jealous of them? How do your actions make you feel? How can you do better?

What is the root cause of your jealousy? Where does it stem from? What limiting belief has led to jealousy?

JEALOUSY

How do you feel when someone is jealous of you? How do you not let their behaviors / actions stop you from living your life?

Write down every single thought in your mind right now about your jealousy. No judgement, just write it all out.

Write 10 affirmations to remind yourself of your value. How can you keep reminding yourself?

How can you accept *(in a healthy way)* that jealousy is a part of your emotional experience and how can you not let it affect the way you treat people / yourself?

How can you take a break / take a step back when you start to feel obsessive / act impulsively out of jealousy?

How can you communicate your jealousy to your partner / friend, etc in a healthy way? How can they support you as you heal your jealousy?

Write 10 affirmations
to help you recognize
the good in your life
when you are jealous
of someone. How can
you keep reminding
yourself of it?

How has jealousy
negatively impacted
you? How do you feel
about it? How would
you like to change it?

Imagine a future
version of you that is
secure in yourself
and not jealous.
How would that
look like?
What would you feel?
How can you get there?

JEALOUSY

Write a letter
to someone you were
once jealous of.
What caused it?
How did you
overcome the feeling?
What would you like
to say to them?

Write a letter
to someone you are
jealous of. How can
you reframe your
mindset and be happy
for them instead?

Write a letter to your
past self who was
jealous of someone.
Show kindness
and forgiveness
for the actions
taken out of jealousy.

What do you define as an insecurity? What are some of the signs unique to you that indicate you are dealing with an insecurity?

What are your thoughts / feelings / behaviors when you are dealing with an insecurity?

Write about a bad experience that led to the insecurity. How can you reframe your takeaway from the incident?

Why do you think you compare yourself with others? Where does that stem from? How can you heal that behavioral pattern?

Why do you feel less than others? How can you make yourself feel better about yourself?

(List accomplishments, achievements, good qualities, etc)

Where do you think you should be today? Where are you now? How do you feel about the difference?

INSECURITY

(Continued) How can you adjust your expectations of where you should be? How can you be accepting of where you are at today?

(Continued) If you were to look at yourself objectively, with no insecurities, how would you feel about where you are at today?

Write about a past failure that led to the insecurity you have today. How can you build trust towards yourself today?

Write exactly how you are feeling about yourself today. Mention every insecurity. No judgement, just document it for yourself.

How has an insecurity affected your interpersonal relationships?

(Write about as many insecurities as you would like.)

How has an insecurity affected your values, beliefs, perspectives and behaviors?

How has an insecurity affected the way you view yourself? How would you like to view yourself? What steps can you take to get there?

What has been the consequences of succumbing to an insecurity? What would you have wanted to do differently?

Imagine taking an action without any insecurity holding you back. What would that look like? What's the first step you can take to get there?

INSECURITY

Write a letter to your past self and honor how difficult it was to deal with your insecurities. Shower your past self with a lot of love and compassion.

Write a letter to your present self encouraging yourself to continue healing your insecurities.

Write a letter to your future self explaining where you are today and where you hope to be someday. *(As realistic as possible.)*

Prithvi Madhukar—aka The Marketing Nomad—is a quirky digital entrepreneur and business owner with a passion for marketing and a zest for life. She is the Author of Zero to Four Figures and Self-Loved. She is also a Podcaster (Top 100 in Marketing—India, Top 10% Global), YouTuber, Etsy Shop Owner, Skillshare Teacher, and Influencer. She is also the CEO of The Marketing Nomad LLC, a global Marketing Consultancy Firm in Delaware that has helped seventy-plus clients from eight different countries as of 2023. As a location-independent Marketing Strategy Consultant, she empowers business owners to confidently implement long-term marketing strategies to grow the business they love. She enjoys Bollywood dancing in her free time.

Prithvi's life story is pretty interesting. She completed her engineering degree only to realize her passion for marketing. After choosing to follow her passion and completing her MBA with a concentration in Marketing, she worked at a top solar firm in New York for a year. When her H-1B work visa was not processed, she was forced to leave the US, which meant she had to leave her fantastic full-time job, amazing colleagues, best friends, and a place she had called home for three years.

Absolutely devastated and desperate to find hope in life again, she decided to risk her entire savings and invest in her dream of becoming a digital entrepreneur in 2019. After successfully finding ways to navigate through her journey, she made it her mission to empower other digital entrepreneurs and business owners with marketing, business, and mindset help to grow the business they love. Her content on all platforms be it her book or her videos, share a genuine and authentic insight into her personal and professional life. It has inspired many to continue pursuing their own entrepreneurial journeys.

As she continues to dive deeper into the entrepreneurial world, she invites you to join her roller coaster ride. If you'd like to know more about her marketing strategy consultation services or catch her on all her social media platforms, you can use this QR code, or you can visit themarketingnomad.co/main

ZERO TO FOUR
FIGURES

broke

LESSONS LEARNED BY A CEO
^

PRITHVI MADHUKAR

BOOK BLURB

After completing her Master of Business Administration (MBA) in New York, a twenty-something Indian girl learns that her work visa wasn't processed.

So what happens when she is forced to leave the United States of America, her best friends, an amazing job, and a place she called home for three years?

I'll tell you—She becomes a CEO and goes by an online pseudonym, "The Marketing Nomad".

In case it wasn't evident, that girl is me.

Through this narrative non-fiction book, I give you a glimpse of the first three years of my digital entrepreneurship journey from Zero to Four Figures. This book is a compilation of sixty-one lessons on topics ranging from mindset to business, marketing, losses, and wins. I share the challenges, mistakes and the strategies that led me to some of my breakthroughs. Don't worry; you'll also get my original models, performance tools, and learning tactics if you'd like to implement those for your journey (Bonus: 50+ page Printable Workbook PDF).

You will also learn what it means to change the narrative when defining your successes and how to break free from waiting to hit six or seven figures to view yourself as a successful digital entrepreneur.

If anything, I know that this book will comfort you that you aren't alone in your journey and show you that somewhere in the world, there's a digital entrepreneur named "The Marketing Nomad", albeit a little quirky, who is cheering you on!

Available on various Amazon marketplaces and online bookstores.
Visit
www.themarketingnomad.co/books/zerotofourfigures for more details.

PLATFORMS

Website:
themarketingnomad.co

Instagram:
@themarketingnomad

Twitter:
@themrktgnomad

YouTube:
youtube.com/c/themarketingnomad

Podcast:
The Marketing Nomad Show
(Available on Apple Podcasts, Spotify, Google Podcasts, Amazon Music, iHeartRadio, Stitcher, and all major podcast platforms)

LinkedIn:
linkedin.com/in/prithvimadhukar/

Etsy Digital Shop
etsy.com/shop/themarketingnomadco

Skillshare:
skillshare.com/user/themarketingnomad